Little People, BIG DREAMS®

SHAKIRA

Written by
Maria Isabel Sánchez Vegara

Illustrated by
Laura Díez

Frances Lincoln
Children's Books

Once in Barranquilla, a Colombian city where music from all over the world met, a girl full of rhythm was born. To honour their roots, her parents named her Shakira, which means 'grateful' in Arabic.

She was four when her father took her to a Middle-Eastern restaurant where a musician played the doumbek, a traditional drum that accompanies belly dancing. As soon as she heard its sound, Shakira felt a warmth in her tummy!

Belly dancing became a way to express herself.
Every Friday at school, she would perform the same dance.
Her classmates were a bit fed up, but she never got enough.
For her, the stage was the greatest place on Earth.

But Shakira was also fascinated by words. At home, she would write poems that became songs. The first, 'Tus Gafas Oscuras', was dedicated to her father, who wore dark glasses to grieve the death of his oldest son.

Impressed by her many talents, her parents took her to singing, modelling and dancing lessons. There, Shakira learned the secrets to becoming the best performer she could be.

Soon, she was performing in talent shows.

Yet all the lessons to be a star were worthless if she didn't learn to be a good person, too. The morning her father took her to a park where orphans lived, Shakira made herself a promise: one day, she would help kids like them.

By the time she was 13, Shakira had recorded her first album. It wasn't very successful, and neither was the next one. Still, she didn't give up, and four years later, when her third album came out, she finally conquered the Latin charts.

Latin music had crowned a new queen! From Colombia and Argentina, to Chile and Brazil, everyone in South America danced to her sound. Shakira was ready to take her music to all corners of Earth, and back again!

But no matter how far her music took her, she never forgot her promise. Shakira created a foundation that brings education and a brighter future not just to the orphans in her hometown, but to Hispanic children all over the Americas.

AMISTAD

EDUCACIÓN

Wherever she went, Shakira was proud to represent Latinos.
Still, she felt like she was a citizen of the world. Shaking her
hips to the sound of Andean panpipes, she released her first
song in English, proving that music had no boundaries.

Shakira mixed English with Spanish, rock with pop, Indian clarinets with Arabic tambourines, old African riffs with fresh new beats... With each song, she invited everyone to enjoy the many sounds and rhythms of the globe.

She was singing the anthem of the football World Cup in South Africa when she met the future father of her two sons.

And she celebrated her 43rd birthday by performing at America's Super Bowl, using her tongue to make ancient Arabic trills of joy.

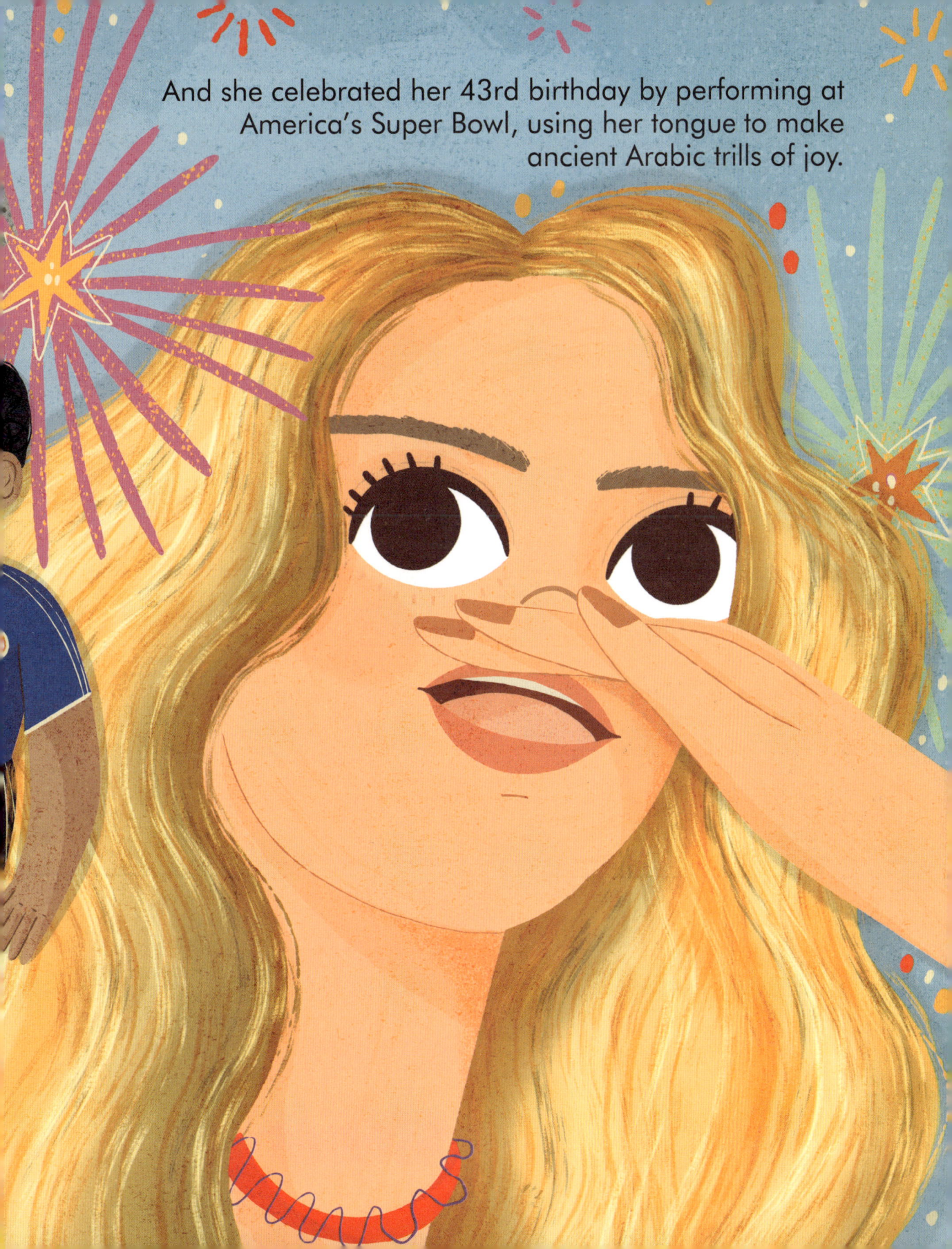

And with more than 140 songs on her hips, little Shakira became one of the most inspiring Latinas that the world has ever met: a unique artist who invites us to move our bodies to the many rhythms of the world.

SHAKIRA

(Born 1977)

2000

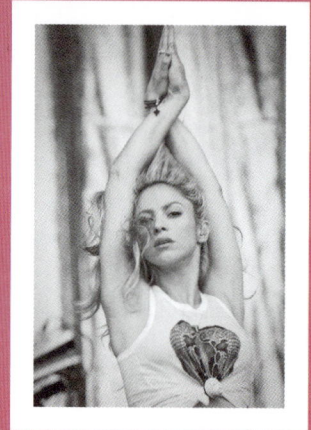

2010

Shakira Isabel Mebarak Ripoll grew up in Barranquilla, Colombia.
Her family experienced tragedy early when her brother was killed in a
motorcycle accident. As a kid, she danced, wrote her own songs and took
part in talent competitions. After singing an acapella audition in a hotel
lobby in Bogotá, Colombia, she was signed to a record label, and she
released her debut album, *Magia,* when she was just 13! After taking a
break from music to act in a soap opera, *El Oasis*, she resumed her music
career with her hugely successful third album, *Pies Descalzos*. The album
sold over four million copies and topped the music charts in eight countries.
Using her fame, Shakira soon formed a charity that was dedicated to
helping poor children in her home country and other Latin American

2011

2022

countries. When she released her first English-language album, *Laundry Service*, she became a household name across the world. During this time, she worked as a UNICEF Goodwill Ambassador and raised awareness of the struggles that children face in developing countries. Shakira has won countless awards for her music, including three Grammy Awards, and has had many memorable performances; in 2020 she was joined by Jennifer Lopez at America's Super Bowl half-time show for a concert that was televised to millions. A queen of Latin Music who brought Spanish-language music to the whole world, Shakira has captured the hearts of her fans with her kindness as well as her songs. To this day, her sunny rhythms inspire people to shake their hips and enjoy the gift of life.

Want to find out more?

Have a read of this great book:

A History of Music for Children by Mary Richards and David Schweitzer

Brimming with creative inspiration, how-to projects, and useful information to enrich your everyday life, quarto.com is a favourite destination for those pursuing their interests and passions.

First Published in the UK in 2023 by Frances Lincoln Children's Books, an imprint of The Quarto Group.

The Old Brewery, 6 Blundell Street, London N7 9BH, United Kingdom.

T 020 7700 6700 **www.Quarto.com**

A catalogue record for this book is available from the British Library.

ISBN 978-0-7112-8309-1

Set in Futura BT.

Published by Peter Marley • Designed by Lyli Feng • Commissioned by Lucy Menzies
Edited by Lucy Menzies and Rachel Robinson • Production by Nikki Ingram
Manufactured in Guangdong, China CC092022

1 3 5 7 9 8 6 4 2

Photographic acknowledgements (pages 28-29, from left to right): 1.LOS ANGELES, UNITED STATES: Latin performer Shakira brought home two Grammy's, one for Best Female Pop Performer and the other for Best Female Rock Vocal performer at the 1st Annual Latin Grammy Awards at the Staples Center in Los Angeles, 13 September 2000. © Vince Bucci/Stringer via Getty Images. 2. GLASTONBURY, ENGLAND - JUNE 26: Shakira performs live on the Pyramid Stage during Day 3 of the Glastonbury Festival on June 26, 2010 in Glastonbury, England. This year sees the 40th anniversary of the festival which was started by a dairy farmer, Michael Evis in 1970 and has grown into the largest music festival in Europe. © Ian Gavan/Stringer via Getty Images. 3. JERUSALEM, ISRAEL - JUNE 21: (ISRAEL OUT) Colombian singer and UNICEF Goodwill ambassador Shakira speaks to Israeli and Palestinian school children during her visit to a Bilingual school on June 21, 2011 in Jerusalem, Israel. The pop star is due to meet with President Shimon Peres and take part in a panel with comedian Sarah Silverman. © David Vaaknin via Getty Images. 4. CANNES, FRANCE - MAY 25: (EDITORS NOTE: Image has been converted to black and white) Shakira attends the screening of "Elvis" during the 75th annual Cannes film festival at Palais des Festivals on May 25, 2022 in Cannes, France. © Gareth Cattermole via Getty Images

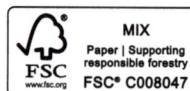

Collect the *Little People*, **BIG DREAMS**® series:

FRIDA KAHLO 	COCO CHANEL 	MAYA ANGELOU 	AMELIA EARHART 	AGATHA CHRISTIE 	MARIE CURIE 	ROSA PARKS 	AUDREY HEPBURN 
EMMELINE PANKHURST 	ELLA FITZGERALD 	ADA LOVELACE 	JANE AUSTEN 	GEORGIA O'KEEFFE 	HARRIET TUBMAN 	ANNE FRANK 	MOTHER TERESA 
JOSEPHINE BAKER 	L. M. MONTGOMERY 	JANE GOODALL 	SIMONE DE BEAUVOIR 	MUHAMMAD ALI 	STEPHEN HAWKING 	MARIA MONTESSORI 	VIVIENNE WESTWOOD 
MAHATMA GANDHI 	DAVID BOWIE 	WILMA RUDOLPH 	DOLLY PARTON 	BRUCE LEE 	RUDOLF NUREYEV 	ZAHA HADID 	MARY SHELLEY 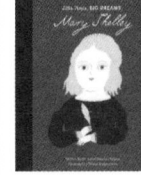
MARTIN LUTHER KING JR. 	DAVID ATTENBOROUGH 	ASTRID LINDGREN 	EVONNE GOOLAGONG 	BOB DYLAN 	ALAN TURING 	BILLIE JEAN KING 	GRETA THUNBERG 
JESSE OWENS 	JEAN-MICHEL BASQUIAT 	ARETHA FRANKLIN 	CORAZON AQUINO 	PELÉ 	ERNEST SHACKLETON 	STEVE JOBS 	AYRTON SENNA 
LOUISE BOURGEOIS 	ELTON JOHN 	JOHN LENNON 	PRINCE 	CHARLES DARWIN 	CAPTAIN TOM MOORE 	HANS CHRISTIAN ANDERSEN 	STEVIE WONDER 

MEGAN RAPINOE | MARY ANNING | MALALA YOUSAFZAI | ANDY WARHOL | RUPAUL | MICHELLE OBAMA | MINDY KALING | IRIS APFEL

ROSALIND FRANKLIN | RUTH BADER GINSBURG | MARILYN MONROE | KAMALA HARRIS | ALBERT EINSTEIN | CHARLES DICKENS | YOKO ONO | MICHAEL JORDAN

NELSON MANDELA | PABLO PICASSO | AMANDA GORMAN | GLORIA STEINEM | FLORENCE NIGHTINGALE | HARRY HOUDINI | J.R.R. TOLKIEN | ELVIS PRESLEY

NEIL ARMSTRONG | ALEXANDER VON HUMBOLDT | NIKOLA TESLA | WILMA MANKILLER | MARCUS RASHFORD | LAVERNE COX | MAE JEMISON | DWAYNE JOHNSON

HELEN KELLER | ANNA PAVLOVA | QUEEN ELIZABETH | TERRY FOX | HEDY LAMARR | SHAKIRA | FREDDIE MERCURY

ACTIVITY BOOKS

STICKER ACTIVITY BOOK | COLOURING BOOK | LITTLE ME, BIG DREAMS JOURNAL

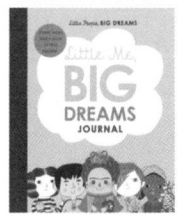

Discover more about the series at www.littlepeoplebigdreams.com